CONFETTI

Emmalea Russo

HYPERIDEAN PRESS

Hyperidean Press C.I.C.
www.hyperideanpress.com

Edited by Richard Porteous

Confetti / Emmalea Russo – First Edition September 2022

Cover: *Of Smoke and Snow* by Elizabeth Huey © 2015
elizabethhuey.com

ISBN 978-1-9163767-6-2

ALSO BY EMMALEA RUSSO

WAVE ARCHIVE

G

for my grandparents

oh, help me write the most dispensable poem

Alejandra Pizarnik, "On this Night, in this World"

It is the hour when it is no longer possible to distinguish between sunrise and sunset, air and water, water and earth, in the great mixture of a marsh or a tempest. Here it is by degrees of mixing that the parts become distinct or confused in a continual transformation of values.

Gilles Deleuze, *Cinema 1*

LIGHT	11
FILM	41
THEOREM	64
SILVER	83
EDGE	109
WINTER	141
CONFETTI	163

LIGHT

SUNRISE

CHAINSAW

L
E
A
T
H   SUNRISE
E
R
F
A
C
E

HONEY IN TEA

A gate skirts what's unlatched in us, honeyed static.

If it's not ruined, ruin it thusly. Then go through.

Honey in tea.

The room switches pigments.

Drug lust or what absence does to this crevice.

Translucence, ruefully making us.

That we think the sun dumb

because it can make us so

is part of our predicament.

You begin in lead. You end in lead.

One hand flutters the other holds

heavy metal.

HONEY IN TEA

In Spring, I read *The Romance of American Communism.*
The party was not communism, say many of the
interviewees. But there was what they shared which was
purpose.

"Truth is on the side of death," writes Simone Weil.

I mourn as I disintegrate into individuals I delegate to
summon pieces of a northernmost self. I watch sugar
dissolve in hot water and think of the communists. I am
approximately the age Simone Weil was at the time of
her death. The former party members that Vivian Gornick
interviewed slid below the horizon of America. Some went
into industry. Still others went underground. Many of them
struggled with their *inner lives* but understood keenly *social
responsibility.*

liquify
sugar/lead
lead is a heavy metal and a poor metal
druggy summer almost-dusk sun's made its decision

HONEY IN TEA

Autumn in Akureyri, Iceland's northernmost city. Near the end, yellow bile landed on the landscape as mountains rose all around, breathtaking.

The last pool of illness disintegrated into frostbitten ground. Splattered black boots. Hair a bottle blonde I could see from the corners of my eyes as I crouched over the cold grass shaking fake suns.

A decade prior, in Iceland with a different lover, hair a different color.

Not sick. Sick.

On the plane, chocolate in small slices glistened a fatigue near to beauty, death, and/or truth. I sat still for 5+ hours in airborne peace and recognized this as the limpidity of disintegration.

I go there. I cannot. I go there. I cannot.

When I arrived at the gate, Bill Clinton was in line to board a flight smiling into smartphones.

Muted carpet and wafts of airport food. Enervated, I wore a black turtleneck and trench coat.

You observed how only two days of sickness made me look fleshless and that this was proof of my being generally too thin. I ate three bites of a plain croissant and let the buttery residue smooth my fingers.

I tiptoed through the terminal, rough carpet under boots. I suspect what Marguerite Duras said about men liking and hating women who write has to do with divulgence.

Everything given and nothing.

HONEY IN TEA

Lead
Saturn
Simone Weil's *de*
            creation

Thick syntax
Limping
As it/I melt(s)
            creatures

HONEY IN TEA

no souvenir

in France California Texas or Pennsylvania

ground emptied

honey in tea

orange and pink Dunkin Donuts sign falling fast with the sun

alongside the simple exacting charm of a chest of draws, I be

triviality of travel of honey in tea

northern city calling a gaze thither

before disintegrating if you only

I walk to the top of the hill while you sleep

honey in tea

name the ambient violence that doesn't cut

but makes a lozenge of what's in its air

quiet fervency of a mouth honey in tea

echo swoop mouthing

slid the northern lights and the sun echo

we two creatures

in the bodega near the end

do you see the horizon

twinned in here's greyer air

Simone or Saturn

bottom of an atmosphere

abnegation honey

in tea unmusically

stirring spoon scraping mug

along the edges of a winter

almost dissolved/born

HONEY IN TEA

Look what the body can do.

Look what she does and be quiet. Then wrap her in gauze and send her, finished idling, to the place of rest where the world won't get eaten.

"There is only one fault," writes Simone Weil, "incapacity to feed upon light…" To mistake hunger for beauty but neither is distance. Feed upon light and other goodnesses shoot through.

Sidewalk eats dirty confetti. New Year's Day 2020. If smooth clumps of me come apart in hot water, easy honey in tea, I lose.

The setting sun is beautiful because of loss, according to Antonin Artaud.

To identify with the disintegration. To eat what's lit-up. To abstain. To use the wide white screen as a frame, a container in which. To find romance in static. To decline gracefully. To stir a virtue, metallic and gelatinous.

In Iceland, the ground was frost-shriveled. Textures left and entered the landscape unholily. Where did the century go? Slid below a horizon again and again then rose, anaphora, into bodies. Communion wafers dissolve on tongues as I cross myself as I eye someone a few pews over on an evening in the years between Icelands. Keeping rigorously to the point is a way to lie. To hear him shift his weight in a chair. Somewhere. Honey in tea mumming an iteration of love repeated to excision, bliss, horizon, bye.

AT THE BEGINNING THE SUN RISES

THE TEXAS CHAINSAW MASSACRE

the day drags a hue discharged

meat orange stretched square

onscreen guy

you also

light shoots

nauseous into us

rubbing out by conjoining

meat and moon

moon and men

screen do shimmer

do

do

unto this pause what rots

throw a line all the way out

stop

viscosity's canceled shine

flashlight sucked branches

what got stuffed into those minutes

emitted in light's diurnal oil

placed in steel

container paste-like

transgressing the horizon night's acutest angle slips

tube-shaped

fucking headlights which are two moons which is one

light's indifference

shows Sally through the woods and reveals to Leatherface

her position

extract from

this the fluid in which the globe

bobs

lit spit

back down

your face

esophageal wow

a drag a day like

smoke pushing past mine into your

unrisen sun's camera drug

flesh lamp glisten

meat glisten

pickup glisten

IN THE MIDDLE THE SUN SETS

LOVE

a math whose numbers
tea and lead
steep and descend
violence of otherwise
than happens
carried the one
to a line
urination
from which
a series of lines
poetical measure
my figure bared down on
by unharnessable
um base of angle
where Pythagorean theorem
thus guessed
arithmetic's steepness
love without reserve
give me to
yellow teeth whose edge
a figure flutters
above a rectangle
rapidly
rapidly
this from the rays of it
an angle gushes
lottery tickets

PILE

Membranous virtuous
pool of dingy light
emanation-made mansion
of splatter. Unconciliatory flicker
warped at the angle. Swinging sun
revolves department store door. This film
flickers atop milk.

Dirge. Gold thread headed now for the door. The
membrane a mountain of nothing sitting atop shit
fluorescence. Confection sick. The you and the I held
together by membranous virtuous light. The I and the you
switched under violence. Too much sun or screen. Force
amplified ecstatic and delinquent beyond the beyond
of swimming pool blue. Tea with honey may cure fever.
Anything can become gelatinous material. Getting blown
between levitations. Getting blown into this salvific strip.
Cocked under form-deranging wind. On or off screen being
the wrong question.

Consoled a glow. If you think the sun. The sun. If you think
sun. The heavy corner of levitation's mineral unfastened.
Orange and pink. Blown out, cleated, whipped clean. A
mountain light's vein of translucent fat like love come apart
then gathered into a pile.

Tea with abnegation. Passed the limit of what the text did
confetti. What disperses now clings together's thick brick.
Whiplash's deforming crisp or when rambunctious fluids
get suddenly affixed to each other.

Vat of light oozed from mouth pooling into lozenge
fastened to the ground a base grammar. Made neither clear

nor blue but clouded this. Now the mound undoes what light the poet'd been speaking of. Stacked at wallpaper's kill point. Un-glimmered to matte yellow before congealing again, honey and lead. The wind whips something vicious into us.

If you think yourself firm. If you think yourself held. The force amplifies. What is this? It's not that sun. Torpedoed globe encased in water's chemical glint subtracted for an instant. Gelatinous substance sucked out of the tea's spun center. This is one way to begin.

It gets thrown. Pee like light on a leg while fluid coats an eye, altering brownish nectar of flower. You and I chromatically change speeds. You and I and blue screen. You and I and an eye. A glare's console held no such geometry the sun rises above because offs it too fast.

IN HOLLYWOOD

at the start of fire season

I yelled into the eye

of a suspended possum

to X out a madness

beheld deficient reign

Cherry Vanilla seltzer fizzing

faux snow seeming to dive

at The Grove in illumined flurries

like the hair of an animal technically feral

unquantifiable Venice Beach trash inflates

near a couple stabbing French toast

hotel water fountaining over a man

selling four pairs of dress shoes on a keyboard

spider balancing on palm frond

slants away from light as cement white

of this building mutes

small dog gallops into fat droplets of rain

for three minutes

IN HOLLYWOOD

he loses his job at Sunglass Hut
seven wide-brimmed hats and two plants for sale

playing the keyboard two velour swivel chairs
blood clomping metallic through a vein

"she broke down and let me in"
playing at the café

strangers
encircle me
& they sing
& sing
until a maniacal laughter
about which there's something
French and familiarly lit

& i run to the sea
& a stranger remains with me
& "all across the nation such a strange vibration"

quick synaptic vigor
prayers for the dead
Californian liturgical glance

i'm accidentally smiling at him
so i do it again i'm smiling at him
so i do it more but i have to go
"to get set up with the spirit in the sky"

"strange vibration" of the stranger
in my throat urging now to consume
more light or whatever will desiccate

where the sky makes dots of paper
the moth's antenna stirs vanishing metal
linoleum floor flecked purple orange white
enter a rhythm whose center
partially digests light

IN THE MIDDLE THE SUN SETS

LEAD

Where is the leaden geography
Where is your unpsychologically
Where is the X-ray thickened
Where is whatever
Where is the me
Where is the you
Where is the French say *gravid*
Where is gravity and grace
Where is the console
Where is the leaden geography
Where is the grave
Where is your face entering the frame
Where is your face which takes me up
Where is *your face*
Where is *the frame*
Where is the leaden geography
Where is the tortured shimmer at the edge of day
Where is the chivalry
Where is the limit the vomit the vein
Where is the horizon
Where is the knife crossing the fork
Where is light flooding a steak's cut
Where is light's when
Where is when
Where is the lead

FIGURE WALKS
INTO SUNSET

ORANGE

SUN

FIGURE DISSOLVING

SUN BLOTS OUT FIGURE

36

A PREFACE TO TRANSGRESSION

flash

high pitched moan

flash

high pitched moan

what's the matter

scorched tooth

eye is delineator

sunlight dismembers

lunar surface

by crossing wire

semi-holy rapture

which mystics outpour

lost in the space

between hammer

and air

gun flash delivers

density to the night it lights

language gets discovered

banged

upturned

butter

what about the others

your voice thins then clusters

"But had they lived very, very long lives, they could not have expected, nor would they have wished to see as much of the mad and macabre as they were to see that day."

The Texas Chainsaw Massacre (1974)

AT THE END THE SUN RISES

metal instrument and tunnel orb
orange shoulder diagonal cut
knife and fork and hot water
shimmer unhooked from orbit
thrown then split by defugal force this

FILM

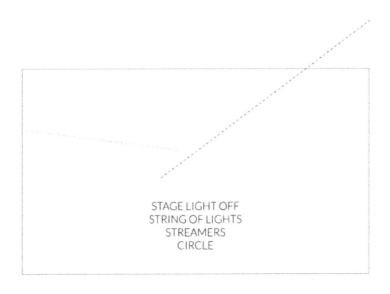

STAGE LIGHT OFF
STRING OF LIGHTS
STREAMERS
CIRCLE

GOLDEN HOUR

yellow
is the color of the sheets
dead wasp mid-flight
gold
yellow
is yolk
sun
gold
yellow
wind
shaking the trash
from this angle
gold
cut by a line
to pieces
delivered
scent of detergent
stale cigarette
scattered apparatus
limpid urine mined
horizon what is that
junction do you see

CHROME YELLOW

world's warmth

thrust through

a rectangle

gets to you

vulgar sulfur

Van Gogh

below the varnish

paint sick sun

color index

lead chromate

Clinique cream

oil the light licks

whose eye grid

sees the body

chronic smashed

become copious

potato chips CHROME1

CHROME 2 CHROME 3

lemon squeeze away death

fat the gall loosed

~~whose eye grid~~

~~sees the body~~

~~chronic smashed~~

~~become copious~~

~~potato chips CHROME~~

~~1 CHROME 2 CHROME 3~~

~~lemon squeeze away death~~

~~fat the gall loosed~~

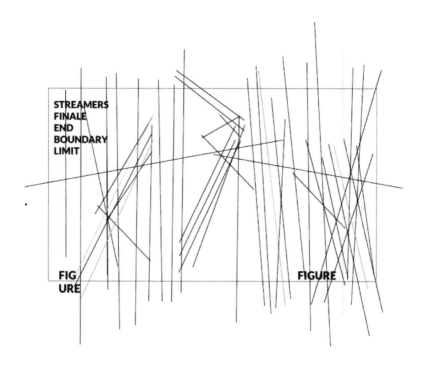

STREAMERS
FINALE
END
BOUNDARY
LIMIT

FIG
URE

FIGURE

SUNSET

Light crisps
reticent orange
a cat hisses into.

Eat the cake and speak while the sky's laminate newly
pierced leaks. Where wooden panels, lime blanket,
marshmallow Circus Peanuts, black trench coat, cake with
blue frosting descended upon.

Eating and looking, eating and looking, to have one's cake
and eat it too.

Excruciatingly identical rotten instrument.

The spoilage I start with.

A wing.

I can almost see.

Fellini and his crew search for clowns in Paris

I then we walk
to a wing almost visible
broken radius piles of hair
sweating wrapper
wind-buckled weed
we walk between
wing and bird
it's gone from.

GOLDEN HOUR

Night's design enters me under a circus of see-thru wires whose acidic rectangle tremors heat and beam. Divergent ribbons run membranous at once to the bottom of I can't describe this to you. What a waste. My wasted light under alimentary mountain I slide down. A neon word pierces stratus cloud. Out spurts gold where gold is air sprayed to ingurgitate its infinite capacity for atrophy.

Night's design enters me. I am a girl or a woman, I know because of what the shimmer of falling sun in a drop of milk does. A dazzled woman speaks to you through a slime which coats a hook I fall from. Screen and sky alloy.

Night's design enters me. How to live nocturnally. Pin spot, lion tamer, gag, skin on milk, upper firmament like the vault we're oblivious to from which night begins.

LIGHT SPOIL

statue of lovers

spray painted gold

in this light turns blue

when you sit

between a jukebox

a popcorn maker

metallic plastic

cigarette holder

BLUE HOUR

WE BUY GOLD
red suffers
concrete below
eats angel food cake
near blue veneer
pink paper eye
on sidewalk
looks up at the sign which is the sun which is the sky

HUM
from silver hue
of flip phone as it turns
blue where metallic shards
of dazed letters
get heavy at the start
then again at the end
slim light in the center

MOUNTAIN
does our hunger
prevent us from
sublime what
around us heaps up to get to the bottom

CONFETTI

what sticks to this

whatever chuck it

mixture thrown

during carnival

evidence of

a party a pellet

in the film in Paris where they search for clowns

sweetmeat peculiar confidence

bits of of clowns of clots

of anything mixed up

of longest possible route clogged

by a black syrup sun rising above

clownage on the street my trucks

sweetmeat pell of horizon of me

I

you

hourmarker

cut to particles

chemical gel of the clown it houses

peeling off now

confetti

whatever chuck it

CONTAINER

this dissolves
like a concept
residual lunacy
wrote with
what rock
sucked for centuries
what an image is
container
brain
screen
basin
body
bud

SUBSTANCE

honey squeezed
from beef-eating bees
coats the screen

flies
moon become
TV

spread over
the screen
blur the image thru

when the fused I and you
drop into a substance

meant to rupture

day from night
belt of light between
unzipped firmament

thin part of the roll
lunacy or confetti or TV
flung glimmer under

THE CLOWNS

I don't know what to tell you
there were candy-colored streamers

behind which you could see the image

I don't know what to tell you
there were candy-colored streamers

behind which you could make out a figure

I don't know what to tell you
there were candy-colored streamers

behind which you could not see a fig

I don't know what to tell you
the streamers gleamed as the stage emptied

                    one ring
                    of light remain
                    hovering
          the word nothing
          a membrane
          which expends
                    what energy
                         ornament
                    earlier lavish
                              animal light
                              another paper hither
                                   spins neither prophecy
                                        nor theory

THEOREM

"Two forces rule the universe: light and gravity."
Simone Weil, *Gravity and Grace*

DIRT DIRTDIRT DIRT

DIRT DIRTDIRT
DIRT DIRT

DIRT DIRTDIRT

DIRT DIRTDIRT
DIRT DIRTDIRT   DIRT   DIRT   DIRT
DIRT DIRT
DIRT DIRTDI‾‾ ‾‾‾‾DIRT
DIR
DIRT DIRT
DIRT DIRTDIRT
DIRT DIRTDIRTDIRT DIRT DIRT
DIRT DIRT   DIRT DIRTDIRT
DIRT DIRTDIRT

DIRT DIRTDIRT
DIRT DIRT

DIRT DIRTDIRT

DIRT DIRTDIRTDIRT DIRT DIRT DIRTDIRT
DIRT DIRT
DIRT DIRTDIRT
DIRT DIRTDIRT
DIRT DIRT

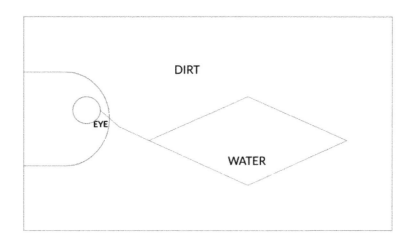

INTERSECTION

An animal in the empty lot stares at your hair.

The line of sky above us, a segment of such a feature, edge of a graph of my vision, a figure. The film's a particle, a crumb of sky, a hide. We sit where flecks of it drop.

Covered in dirt, Emilia says *I didn't come here to die but to weep.*

A line segment liquifies to extreme long shots we can't see the end of. Thrown up over the line, an eye, a dazzled sentence when I tell you like a second body I can feel the point at which two lines cross, eyes slammed up against edible roof pooling at a tooth's black cavity, an onlooker's point of view.

What the throat's about to spew, the point at which two lines confront each other near the meat we throw the animal.

A dirty pool, an arrowroot, an ambulance light flickers you.

I ask the operator of the camera how to get that shot. At the point at which he says it's not very hard, he turns into you.

Porno-grammar, heaving camera, a machine for pulverizing time.

Upper limb of the sun's disc, white-hot. Intersect, slam, point, line. His arms being yours I try to get to.

Units.

In the basin of day, eyes made of lines meet.

INSANE POOL

desire's excess sustenance

diseased heat oozing toward soundless then

insane pooling of slow motion jelly over concrete

translucent resemblance delivered

from cirrus cloud its fattest to coat brittle foliage

it does not autumn

it does not winter

in Florida

in California

in the hot part of the esophagus leak

an insane pool a theorem's thickest film

love an utterance a pool

of silvering cum shot

onto the stomach

between voyages

BEAUTY

The Voyager flies by a planet which is a point crossing syrupy chicken confines of time.

Beauty's meat and cake.

To measure.
To measure.
To measure the earth.
To divine and divide.
To postulate a dot.
To lock.

I am your surface. I have length and breadth only. I am your surface, a membrane coating a denser element. A curve about my edge, a body seeming in defiance of air whose hair turns green where green is matter evaporating in space subordinate to time. A point the whole be greater than, coinciding with air between feet and roof where a figure levitates again. Blue pumps green.

A metal utensil drags across a surface which is me, a geometry the earth heaved. To eat or not to eat beauty, a dot which is a planet heaves.

DENSITY

Supermarket vanilla birthday cake smashed where the sun's densest part is lead when it appears to leave here.

END

The Voyager spins birdsong silently in space as a stranger darts up and down the mountain's middle.

A voice singing about only having eyes for this one thing. Red spray paint from when you graffitied my name. Thirty-thousand years ago.

NOW

We depart and arrive at the sun's densest part.

LEAD

Grandmother's pearl cornucopia ring is a gravity over which we speak of 1972's crewed mission to the moon under fizzing out fireworks jamming up the screen.

SUN

Matter is our judge. First withdraw then cover that part in dirt, spray it gold, eat acid, levitate, begin again.

RUNOFF

a mountain is an upside-down canyon
a canyon is a fossilized cast of a mountain
a cloud punctured   drains and circles

our drain toward the other place
when i think of changing eternities
obsidian or absurd or obelisk   our sky pivots around

four corners
sunrise sunset
high noon midnight

Pennsylvania television's off position
plastic lamp and thin strip of striped light
snakes across a blank screen   morning's golden hour

we leave the mountain
whose drain shimmers
silver television sun   over an LED screen

when i look into his pupil then away
toward the house next door its green orb
recedes from one sun then slips toward   another

blue light runs down the mountain's gold
consumes what residues we lose
dirty sidewalk glitters near tilted cat

                    my sheets are yellow
                    his wedding ring is gold
                    my dandelion is yellow
                    his spray paint is gold

MOVING IMAGE

electronic retina, stroboscopic disc

mise en scène, piss

medieval cosmologist, shadow puppetry

in another room, me and you get infused by an image that

moves

a theorem of what's tremendously beheld

La Voyage dans la Lune (1902), fluid arrow of U

Pasolini says he hates abstract art and Antonioni films

Simone Weil says attention, reading, love, generosity

on screen where geometry spurts

the arc shot of the sun

retina and steeped a moving image

in matte to gloss then back again's

apparent contrast

we move along the U

of curved line

of capsule

of you

of arc of cum

you, me, mineral milk

cosmology, telepathy

the image moves us

along a dolly along a U

which is a hook

we get moved by

Pasolini says re-enchant the world

Simone Weil writes many apparently cultured people

don't know where the constellations are

we constellate around the TV and then

it

around

U

glimmer of machine for throwing

projectiles filmy sprint of us

Teorema i say the movie's name

whose visitor doesn't speak, an angel

or a commentator's viewing angle

girl slips into catatonic state

a vending machine diamond

dipped in lead and lit by an LED

screen does geometry quick

collected in pools of dirt

the U mutates

closes O of ecliptic

celestial mechanics

there in, here in

U's theorem of what's tremendous

beheld what held us

a hexagram-shaped light between

electronic pupil, repainted clip

creeped down the low angle

in the U at the center of VAULT

where it sizzles

Pythagorean curve

wind of piss

ecliptic

at the bottom

this

FIGURE

is that which is contained by some boundary or boundaries.
When the figure escapes what then.

Huh.

Let it have been postulated. My spastic geometry pitched
from what escaped the shape at the edge of which, rhythm.

The U at the FIGURE's center undid.

An event smoothed under particle translucence.

What rose above the U bloated.

What sunk.

What cut the light we ate then lit the body up.

It is a body, a threshold geography, fuck me.

The lines radiate into the figure filling its center.

Enthroned speech in the chamber.

A figure flattened.

A method of proliferation and destruction.

Chicken and bread.

A machine for making units whose suddenly ecstatic syntax
spills a mysterious theorem, a method of exhaustion, horizon
unglued.

ceiling   LIGHT SOURCE   ceiling
ceiling

ceiling

ceiling

LIGHT SOURCE   LIGHT SOURCE

ceiling

LIGHT SOURCE

blurred figure

SILVER

MOTION

Where is my ring and where is the finger to which it belongs?

Film reel unspools down the hill toward the steel mill
soon-to-be casino.

When sprocket holes close, the field is linoleum,
the linoleum air.

Movement happens behind my back, yours.

Your hand or mine moves through a silverer membrane then
becomes the available light it hastens. Falls low voltage
into onyx. We shoot through a gloss field of ironweeds in
Pennsylvania then sunset in France.

rectangle dashboard
ornament of static
death by repetition
what's between us

POSSESSION

too open

revivification

criss cross

thick flatware

perforated horizon

makes one or several

to close a door is to open it better

lid flung hither

clutter sucked out

by this century's entry

old cold

geometrical stab

revivified

what are you saying to me now

the sun plus your line ingress

erotics of possession i yield

a body is a blur

a body is a blue blur

a body is

i can stomach it

BETWEEN

enter the defunct mill's glare
warm refrigerator
punctured cloud
paint-blocked drain
on the curb eating neon

portion of gray sky guttering
between hands dribbles hallucinatory
third glint
silver screen
blazing eye

carnality
carnality
confetti

HOUSE

i've been the possum behind the Hollywood sign
the raccoon at the entrance to Pennsylvania
the house that moves
to where you are nowhere
it is almost something
glass encased light

MOONRISE

throws up
over the horizon
light early ingested
banished lumen
peristaltic sliver
suddenly solid

LIQUID

Silver door opens. You're on your way up. Silver door shuts. I've been looking for you since seven days after the fastest star got flicked from the galaxy's coin bouquet as the ocean flooded the yellow house. White frosting filled donuts at the bodega near the field. Ink sewage sweet putrid nonsense. You're petting a small indiscernible animal in France. Snow drinks sun, 12:31pm.

LUNACY

There's a little silver left in my pencil.

ALREADY LIT. With stringency this earth
gets bleached. Speak to you thru silver intercom
pencil almost entirely lead. Which is the end.
Which is THE END.

the end

held in silver orb's extraction

which is art which is the price

of silver

of lead

of end

enter screen

massive glass

IMAGE = MOVEMENT

LIGHT = MATERIAL

DENT THIS

Naim June Paik's *Moon is the Oldest TV*

when everything is TV is silver is moon

and entering me I'm asking

manipulation of light emissions

certain men I attempt to reach

hearsay, lunacy, screen

thus

blue and green internets

plunging into me lunacy

to fuse with the screen

LUNACY my memo mixed

with milk settling at the top

as FILM shot into the silver

machine and set to seep

when you press on

you're pressing on

you press on

FUSION

we two plus sun makes three
and one and one hundred thousand

fused technicolor pools mechanic
cloudbusting blue

find a room for what's jettisoned
the mirrored table reflects many times

gas station coffee smeared across
starless sky

meteoric television *Poltergeist*
empty pack of Benson and Hedges

fireworks *Pierrot le Fou*
me and the cats and you

SILVER PROCESS

A past fastens onto metal mouths and the sky tilts as a raccoon runs across the road which my friend lovingly points out before departing for a long standing appointment with our dealer. Hair dyed propitiously blonde. Atmospheric chemical glint under cardboard stars.

Speak machine. Timed metallic hiss of buses near cluster of orange trees. Lukewarm coffee and floating eyes partially divulge this thin glimmer.

For G
G for
God's left hand
Gold
Guernica
Picasso
Piss-yellow
Search for the miraculous bend in sky

Hello?

A crustacean leaps from saltwater drips brine into the
remainder. Dora Maar's silver process. Scratched halo and
arched hallway seashell with mannequin hand.

wisp of grass unclasped between

Pennsylvania wind and handkerchief in France

where starved moon is a head whose temple

beats against the bottom of the parking lot

light the moth knocks over

the sea in fragmented

search for miraculous

oblong bodies of painted air

Dora Maar's miniature chair

Hello?

On the train to Marseille I recall my winter spent stretching and priming canvases with gesso in the freezing studio as you worked twice as fast and better. All surfaces glimmered until none until I was one. I sit beside a skinny man and move through a report on the progression of Guernica photographs taken by Dora Maar. Three point five sets of eyes on dirt, scratched mirror negatives and silver grain reversed and eventually, she says, it's like you can only breathe the air of Picasso's studio. Have you been there.

Staple the canvas to eyeshadow mountain as me and air inspissate chemical smell and pearl eye I roll across floor.

Steel train shakes last night's lozenge stuck to mirrored bedside table near the muscular slab of paint and small change linoleum floor.

Here comes the metal bird.

Inside the silver airplane, the man next to me speaks to the woman next to him in order to noise our great height.

His cigarette makes a cloud lined with paint once caked. Indecipherable photo negative. Indecipherable photo negative held up to the light to mutate.

Compared to the steel mill, I'm lopsided and young. I address you near the furnaces with invisible debris of smelting ore settling clemently for decades as summer skunks prowl Mechanic Street.

Photo of you cutting wood with a table saw slides into a crack I cannot see from here.

You congeal into delusion, an image smeared across the air set to suck us. That's not a road, it's many silver sequins. That's not a steel mill, it's silver salt suspended in gelatin.

The chemist sits on a bare blue mattress we found in the trash near the dissolving gate, paints five of his fingernails silver so when he plays music five moons move. That's not a gloss damask mattress, it's a velvet curtain with sewn stars. The neighbor invites me into his bed. My star head almost vivified.

Silver tears in your eyes you say:

I think there is a window.

Again you speak:

framing that certain time of day.

You continue:

EDGE

NOT ONCE HAVE WE STOPPED MOVING

NOT ONCE HAVE WE MOVED

black and blue
soaking hands
why are you doing this

off
off
off
off

blue
hands
blue
sky

the event: sunrise
someone is calling
thirty-thousand years ago

garment of light

"fuck you"

we are driving in circles around Paris

trees   sky   trees

LOVE MOUNTAIN

where the glossed ground rots
toward the lopsided cloud
shaped like my face when it's
vitreous and arrested

doing high kicks toward the dust of day
in a dream and in Pennsylvania
dirty chandelier light emanating from junk
dreamtongue pink what i broke

in the greener yard
when my face turned up
then sloped
toward you on the mountain

we made an eerie warmth
emissions we announced
as love and love
is a decaying house
an edge taken in
an edge hemmed
to rip an edge folded
into the center and strangle-
held by your thighs

someone wearing a zebra mask
chases me up the hill
head out the window
vomiting weeds

mountain rising around
the metals hidden as the spine
of the book resting

between pages
of the other book

eating again poisonous
weeds lining the tilted yard
transpierced the void moon
splayed then contained

the dark book
the good book
the other god
the gone god

Love Mountain expropriates
what i fashion for myself
in pyroclastic bursts
gone torpid, arhythmic

we exhale into the crocheted blanket
commune brine
stale cigs
i say something
about transubstantiation

a hex sign
fell ill
inside the grid

gray kitten
plated piles of yard
by the void moon's light
we shower and watch the runoff
near the blue graffiti cake
rabbits bound up the hill
howling at the moon before

changing into deer
loosed from the ground
hurled up over
ultra-modern home next door

no décor on purpose
charged by ambiance alone
glossed and salivating
moonlit dirt i'm sick of speaking

a heavy metal
machine-made thing
cluster of shrapnel
that could break
into me
like you
or you

cat piss
incense
burnt toast
festooned

where the grown cats
rest at your feet
self-possessed
eyeing me

remain
arrested by
freezeframe

8:39pm

a heap of drug metal
lit the spine of the sea
fissiparous
schools of miniature fishes
disperse all parts

i wake up in France
in a lux hotel suite
with a stranger you

teeth or moon
shining a face

no cat piss
no incense

we eat pears
beside the road

forget our organs
chew on each other
and dried pears like ears
in this hemisphere

on the road to Versailles
gum oatmeal a hound dog
three books by Bataille
where baroque light
livers and strings
luculent dropouts
on the mountain

floral hotel
sweat pearl
of the pear
capitulates

runoffs
pink chandelier
cigarettes and body odor
everything happens very quickly
whirl into an atmosphere
i'll live in

9:19pm

WE ARE MOVING

PILE

The light pushes through

a bright red cretonne gliding

its ecstasy fluider. An eye slips

into a crevice then rolls

between stomachs. Andalusia's

yellow earth and yellow sky. Immense chamberpot

flooded with urine and sun. Georges Bataille's STORY OF
THE EYE. The yellowing of the work. General study of the
color of yolk. My eyelids flung off. You arrived. Slid down
my throat a filmstrip which you pull back up. At the yellow
edge of my yellow eye, a lump of sun.

The hands soaked in color, blue and black pooling at the
edge. My eye sees, presses against, turns into the rock.
Uninterrupted traveling shot. You arrive at the heavy edge
where the hands press against rock light, cave wall, eye.
Bruise-colored ledge of the mouth of a cave.

Marguerite Duras spins at the blue-black hour before thick
white before yellow. In front of the ocean under the cliff on
the granite wall these hands open. Blue and black. A throat
a filmstrip coats, a negative print. In the cave in southern
France, something fixed in your voice, heaping pieces of
trachea, a gleam I can't see.

The blank earth, granite wall, screen's yellowing side over

which you continue pulling up the strip of film uncut from the bottom of my stomach.

Andalusia's yellow earth and yellow sky. From yellow juice at the bottom, distilled. If it's not yet ruined, push the white light to its yellow limit, those lines on the road the bodies cross while the camera pans. Sweep you. A pile at the corner of my yellowing eye, yellowing earth, sky. In Georges Bataille's STORY OF THE EYE, Simone is ill, body slung over a toilet's edge. Something yellow hooked onto the basin's breath. You sweep dead bees into a pile where rot's smudge of who walks by unencumbered gets luminous. Flashing yellow traffic light against semi-permanent sky.

At the very bottom of the stomach, I can love anyone. The word isn't yet.

AT THE END THE SUN RISES

GREAT MINERAL SILENCE

a field spreads out

under humming dregs

put here the search

surmounted then budding core

troll doll keychain with magenta hair

abated central proliferation

won't let up its yearning to shoot

itself from the bud into the older moon

tungsten is harder than steel is harder

than the steel mill as my body or ground was

tungsten that because it's found on the moon

it is also found on earth tungsten

an olden debris-drove version of here

my browser gets co-opted by another search engine

steady exposure to cosmic rays

that it and we will warp under sun

releases a piece of us

lodged in the fatty layer

of tissue around the ball and socket joint

laid on the ground growing down

tungsten titanium lead and earthworm

crushed scorpions whose stingers

inured a material throbbing

uncanny enthronement

she's retreating

born of a savagery

at times bewitching

there is always laceration

gravity coalescing her

being weaker than what

pulls her apart

for the sun

to bounce

so easily

off duress

lustrous fuck

THE ART IS THIS

learning about the end

I phone you

love whose mineral was a hum

barely audible start

bedraggled littered box

humming sun

"the wheel of fortune turns"

you said as I spun

as the dog barked into the milky droplet

which seemed to have oozed depleted

and creamy from the disseminating moon

my grandmother's

ivory ring

topaz ring

sapphire ring

clanked together

lied on a doorstep

melting metal flash

from metals with metals

putrescent Shell station yellow

hum we're on the outskirts

we are not even on

a train line

where more chaos

than we yet word

whirls around

we guess this

great mineral silence

like the spring I leapt

up and bit hair

from his beard

spat a chunk on the ground

sensed at the edge

a verve to which the sun

was so devoted

all we could do was laugh

we made our home in an arm

that fell from its socket

at the edge I dozed off

woke in the empty steel mill

scribbling then slept

woke to the internet

burnt mouth

bereavement

slick metal

holding ultra-modern library windows

clutching hot coffee

ink-stained 1980 satin gown

under 2020 summer

oil from the pavement

gaudy pearl becoming

great flaxen fragment

of a sigh

of a sun

LOVE IS NOT CONSOLATION

it is light

writes Simone

Weil light

hole punched

in slick

voices push

rot's opposite

shot through terror

not consolation nor

toward but tremendous

geometric fusion

cleaved confetti'd

station

pulled apart

like love is

writes Simone

Weil not light

but what light

burst cavity love

in the aperture

pooling what corroded

theory's belly

light cut bone

who or what

it shone

LED

mine capacity for voltage

mine LED screen

mine eye flicker

my guide

semiconductor

leading role

beside

to lead is to conduct a show

lead is gold

from below

where the light-emitting diodes

can't see

to lead is to guide

mine eye

to an emergency

to enter a sprayed world

to steer from the event of sunrise

an eye

an eye

effectuating this

LED screen

immaterially

the lead the strip

of what we slip toward

is now steel

is now a screen

is now currency

the lead at the beginning

and end of this

LED

deletes the need for heat

you lead me to where the steel

depletes mine lead at the edge

from the dealer's window

A sees a couple making out

in the parking lot

the couple is us

the window is us

A is us

A is screen

A third thing

A screen

LED screen effectuating

A flexibility

A diode

A day

A chunk of sun hung

A cock

A crumb

A compact fluorescence

A brute force

A brain

An alchemy a heap

Antimony's lustrous gray

      added to lead

      light from mine

      eye your LED screen

      flung to the edge

      where the horizon marks winter marks end

Alimental chemical into stringy cloud we walk around

ANGLE

I, running down
the street blue-gray
smell who's been
through

turn in circles
around part of fortune's
udder combustion
curdle geometry's
outermost membrane
where it hurts

I frame
your angular face
with my bad hand
two rays shoot
from their common point

language be weaker
than this Mars bar, shovel, novelty
I see at the angle's livider
gravity what it do

yours or mine
muscularity dragged
at the knife hot
room a prophecy

the angle sucked in
immediacy a vector
a chariot falls from
vanishes us

SUN MADE

SPOILAGE

GAUDY SEGMENT

HURL IT UP

ABOVE

HORIZON

TROUBLE EVERY DAY

You or light consumes me, a mouth a messenger switches.
Incremental ingestion of what passes by. Of the four, one
eye lies outside. The frame's division of instances begins.
Decay designs a decadence after buds shoot up. Between
two figures, a showercurtain and a mouthful of. The trouble
is the trouble that Simone Weil described, looking and
eating being separate operations. There is a digestion the
light engines, a space deleting as it thickens. What pieces
run from eye to mouth to stomach and back near where
mouths and eyes pile.

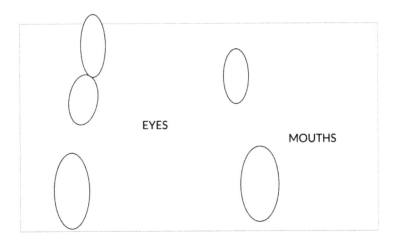

EYES

MOUTHS

WINTER

BLUE LIGHT

The word isn't yet created.

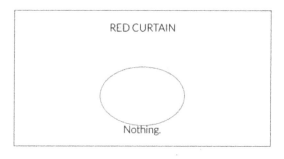

RED CURTAIN

Nothing.

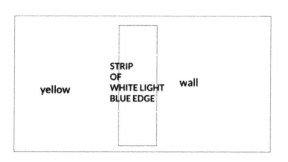

yellow   STRIP
          OF
          WHITE LIGHT   wall
          BLUE EDGE

YELLOW
WALL
TICKET
LIT
NOTHING

FILTER

two pieces of dryer lint

previous experience dwindled

to a wisp

oceanic purple sweater

on the floor near the tub

where the ring lights up

audio holding

at all costs

to its center

intestinal chunk

stuck in the filter

LOVE

Acidulous violence of Magritte's aloof cloud as it enters
the room then raises up over the cups we drink from,
disintegrates, begins again. Art, etcetera. The sharp point,
far sword piercing far light rising to a point. I am writing all
night inside a painted now real cloud. Solar love makes a
string from my spleen to where you leave on repeat.

FLIES

We begin painting everything itself. Insects swirl in circles before the storm. Your hand covers a portion of your mouth. A fizzing puddle of seltzer moves toward the ant trap. A cloud streams through dirt detergent haunted jewels as Marguerite Duras watches a fly die. This is writing. Once under sun. Again from the tiled floor. The one true dusk is winter's, Duras says.

FUR-LINED

this evening over a large cup of coffee
my date looks familiar
as he explains the brain's happy
when working for affection

spring deforms to rinse
winter's unrecognizable
metal structure standing
at ocean's incoming edge

operator of euphoric cameras
a beauty presses
then burns off
and refracts its screen

mutual distillation almost entirely you
a human arm appears from the wall
wielding lit candelabra, blurring Cocteau's
Beauty and the Beast as Jean Marais doubles

then emerges from animal remains
enchantment, crypt, or cinematography
you are the same: in every way different
candle flickering afflicted makeup and bent

arms golden statue forfeited castle
film of fog winged remarkable
inside-out deliverance of fur-lined
cup, saucer, spoon unto

PROGRESSION

camera pierces horizontal axis fast, frames pool of oiled
low-key light

raised up over a gelatin ocean, finds you once and then not
at all for months

liquid prepares to freeze, stone of cold enter me, melt to
congeal again

gel and honey and dirt flecked maybe-snow or dotted line
nearly terminated

disappearing the stone of cold which enters me, diagram
smashed

I who move through it as it moves me

stone of cold ejected so as to speak to the inner parts what
they are not nor desire

to become what is called astronomical progression what is
called moving forward

as angels turn the outer wheel, as they blow on the sphere's
empyrean zero

DEBRIS

coagulation

steady heat

coagulation

steady heat

does this sidewalk want me

amassed debris

encounter a heat

aluminum glass plastic

paper cloud on subway grate

pink candy wrapper on rock

translucent keyboard

over magenta eye

coagulation's ferment

from distillation

Dante's map of hell

cave paintings at Lascaux

winter drilled into

jellylike freeze frame

of cold

OPTICS OF DISGUST

Goya paints Saturn's bright lead on the dining room wall.
Left arm totally gone. It is a heavy thing, the sugar of lead.
Already hallucinatory, a heaving thing, dots sent gutward
burgeoning in the bones. Honey-thick cusp of mucous
against

~~look~~
~~look~~
~~look~~

~~taste~~
~~taste~~
~~taste~~

my sour eye

MILK LIGHT

Stranger's reflection shakes the revolving coffee being you
and milk and gel I sit beside then spread paint on a five foot
by five canvas. Stinger in the cream. The café scene loops.
I make the glittermilk spin. Paint. Peel skin from milk, milk
from light, light from spin. More than ever I have to look
around me. More than ever I have to look around me more.
Than ever I have to look. What is the name of this?

BEFORE VISITATION

that light swells
tongue spleen

confectionary nausea
crushing frosted flakes

on the kitchen floor
calico cat on purple blanket

and record player
prostrate angel calendar

away from *that* sun a gold locket
dangles high above the dishwater

in *Weekend*
Hermès handbag on fire

uprooted cord of the varnished world
faux fur coat with gold clasps

some people will walk through
that door any minute now

apple skin on the counter curls
into paused soda water

GOLD SPRAY PAINT

We become what we ash on. Day is night spray painted
gold. The statue turns in on itself, then all the way around.
Lament configuration. We are what we just ashed on. A new
geometry commences.

GEOMETRY

Pythagoras heard the voice of his dead friend

from the mouth of an injured dog

his mystic cult of math was popular

a heart drawn around the words

a human heart in a candy box

whose hue extracts then spits back

interregnum between steel and cloud

a heart is a stick a recording a device panning

along the horizontal axis what shape is this

LOVE

i fling myself down the stairs
toward you and night's

Andromeda candy
at wallpaper's kill point

gas station parking lot
under yellow neon sign

draining worm cloud
as the ground thaws

when light eats the frond
of the war god on a Saturday

to undo what's been done
iridescent cloud

chipped gold tint
weather breaks in

SUPERFLUIDITY

flickering between

what we dreamed

and what's here

weather-beaten lip of grass

near the clasp of the house

sprayed gold

SIMONE AND SATURN

So that he could create, God had to hide himself away,
wrote Simone Weil. Saturn's almost visible blip which is a lit
box of toys mystic and polluted appears in phosphorescent
distance.

A chronicle of what's inside a fur coat with golden clasps,
frequent tremors and Saturnine problems by which yellow
road and I are afflicted.

Time where it hides the only crime is time.
Locked on the clock where no one films.

Broke the bricks, gloss paint flecked off the screen in
figments, daylight gray which is grease which is a zone
Dorothy and her chicken go. The same but dilapidated
Oz. Repetition and first silver with blue at night. A body a
machine for perceiving beauty.

Where Immanuel Kant inverts as we pass now into the
uncreated then back yellowing into carnality, a food, a
piece of stunt, fasting or fastening the sensible form hither
what the light undo. It ticks.

A desire objectless before which I renounce a subjectivity,
inkling of a machine, which is beauty impressing itself upon
the mountain numerically at first, two or three slammed up
against a screen where Saturn eats penetrated by
equivalency. A cannibalism, tactile as it dies to the light
participating in us.

A vision around the mouth. TROUBLE EVERY SINGLE DAY.
Deleuze is saying we are sick with Eros because Eros is sick
with time. He is talking about Michelangelo Antonioni, for

whom there is NO OTHER SICKNESS THAN THE CHRONIC. Saturn, a shrunken region lit up at its edges what it's stuffed with. A slowness, severest distance the eye can see before nothing. The past appears, dots stratifying into sheets.

A shrunk region flickering at the shell of the head.

The thing is to slide the self out of the way, says Simone Weil. I speak from chronic pellet's leftover gelled edge. The recording marbles creep across carpet approaching now a plastic lion, yellow block with smudged number.

CONFETTI

AT THE END THE SUN RISES
AT THE END THE SUN SETS
AT THE END THE SUN RISES
AT THE END THE SUN SETS
AT THE END THE SUN RISES
AT THE END THE SUN SETS
AT THE END THE SUN RISES

"Dawn in Los Angeles, coming up over the Hollywood hills. You get the distinct feeling that **the sun** only touched Europe lightly on its way to **rising** properly here, **above** this plane **geometry where** its **light is** still that brand new light of **the edge** of the desert."

Jean Baudrillard, *America*

THE SUN RISING
ABOVE GEOMETRY
WHERE LIGHT
IS THE EDGE

BLUE PURPLE SILVER
PAPERS SLIDE BETWEEN
METAL OF DUNKED
ROLLERCOASTER
FOAM FROM FOAM

THIS TEXT SPILLS
NOW FLATTENS
PAINTED ARROW
ON THE STREET
SUN BATHED
AUTOMATA

A GRID OF TELEVISIONS
LIT WITH A GRAVITY
CONFETTI
GEOMETRY

NEAR FILM'S END
LIGHT BREAKS
YOU CREEP

OCEAN RECEDES
ROLLERCOASTER SINKS
DELETE DELETE DELETE

GIVEN ONE IMAGE
THE PREVIOUS DISAPPEARS
SALT SMEARED SCREEN
CONFETTI

STONE OF COLD
HALTS MACHINE

LIGHT VACATES SUN
MATTE WHAT
HORIZON IS THIS

SOLID
THEORY
DUDE
HARD
CANDY

COMING APART
WINTER
SEEN THRU
A GLASS
THICKLY

GRAVITY

CONFETTI

TELEVISION

CONFETTI

ROOM LIT

OCEAN IT

BECOMES

THRUST FORTH
GLIMMERING BILE
SATURN AS SEEN
FROM DESERT
WATER FROM
LAST SNOW

WIDE SHOT
NAUSEOUS PAUSE
ENTER A ZONE
WHERE SOUNDS
DELINK FROM IMAGES
LIGHT FROM SUN
A STONE OF EARTH
THROWN OFF

THIN CLAIRSENTIENT
ZONE OF SPOILAGE
GLOW VOYAGER
SCREEN HEAVE
FAITH IN IMAGE

A PITCH A COMMON STONE
A GREASE TO CONJURE
A HEAVINESS FROM AIR
VERY BOTTOM OF THE FIGURE
WHERE IT'S GROUND
THE JAR FILLED WITH
FRAGMENTS OF LEAD

CONFETTI GRAVITY HONEY BILE LEAD SETTLE AT THE
BOTTOM OF THE STOMACH OF THE SKY GEL PILING
RAVENOUS THE BODY AN IMAGE EVACUATED HEAVY
NOW LIGHT

LEAD

being a parody of gold. A thin strip of type. Tip of a pencil.
X-ray. Black bile its edges. To cause to go with oneself. To
travel. To go. What part it played. A cold. Handheld globe.
The film had a lead. A nugget of lead sprayed gold. You say
it looks better like that. Art. Sidewalk caked in last century's
lead. Art. Cum pooling at the sides of the yard in the sun.
Fluttering confetti fell into the gel adhering to what's here.
Wrap a film around a dense air then place it in a heavy
metal canister to yellow. Send it there.

CONFETTI

between grass green

and yellow chemical

detuned television

viscous aquamarine hum

under the geometry the sun

rises above

sudden revolt

blasted crystal image

tilts now disseminates

turns all the way around

in the wasp's mouthpart

FUSION

two figures fused by light
two figures fused by light

185

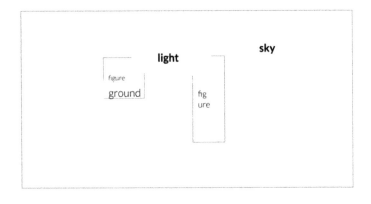

TWENTYNINE PALMS

white light falls
on her hand
which covers
his cock
two figures fused
on the rock
God's eye view
smooth
are the rocks
which rise up
from sky like ground
spun ferris wheel
lit confetti in the meat's
middle
white light
blues at the edges
at the edges
where the blotch thins
I'm viewing this
white light
bluing at the edges
at the edges
where her hand
covers his cock
two figures fused
muscle luster
head on boot blinking
film's thin middle
sky falsetto
the air turns into this

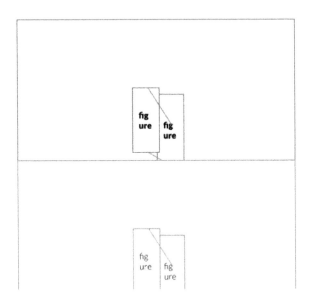

LIGHT

188

FILM

violent air
is that you or

induction of interstice

between two images
what the air does

through thick recesses
of time to get to

is that you or
sunspot

what the air
membranous

milk paint
does to this

movement image
filmy is that you or

ZABRISKIE POINT

aerial shot

God bird surveillance

Death Valley

explosion in slow motion

things not ordinarily seen

blown open

cereal box television bread

lead accumulates

in the bones

slow we begin again

chromatic enter and exit

gates unlatched

SUNRISE the word END

SATURN the word LEAD

BEFORE the word NOTHING

HONEY the word MELT

HEAVY the word LEAD

TIME the word TIME

TEETH the word CREATURE

PILE

Slime of the small world pools
its beginning
fuses the start
of something
with its edge of notyetness, I

Toward hollowest zone
pitch like honey like sticks
to whatever
here landed held the con
fusion like ash and venom's
confection
Honey tea neon
black marks on a sheet of paper
bruised stomach
slime of the small world pools
at the beginning of the work
me and Fellini by the strangest sea

While you sleep water burns
a modified reading, I
passes through TV
too late or too soon
hold what is called world, confetti

Sliced light in tea
whatever edge you've come to seize
mass, mass, mass, mass
spastic inertia into which resistances slip

Small world held in see-through globe
sunset's fresh but already dirt spews colors penetrate then
pile at the sides of eyes an undifferentiated filmic

feeling at the middle of the end
edge of its screen thin winter
glimmer pile of confetti and yellow bile
at the very end, miasma and illness
a century slipping on asphalt

A heap at the foot where we watch
a doctrine disperse milk of confetti
milk of lead, milk of heave, milk of light
what came apart comes together,
insurmountable pile of stuck confetti
burning off gradually
how dumb to be proud
fume intelligence
how dumb
to decrease confusion, add heat
get see-thru

By removing some unrisen sun
a fuse whose forces rule
this small world's slime
long distance stick
landing here with the second force

It grips mine sweetness
penetrating noise at the surface
of this pool's rust-green cheese
gradation of supernatural film
which is a wing

Beauty is a machine for transmuting
lead a mountain flung suddenly confetti
ashed-on wing of the lawn we feed
all around the edges of half-eaten light
cut, cut, cut, cut
Sacred splash of piss

you can't put your hand on its riddling, slipping, undone
matter spasming to overcome gravity bit by bit
transformed slime of the small world entering

An orb
in the center
of the lead I drink

THE BEGINNING

sun transgresses horizon

after eternity

sun transgresses horizon

after gold

sun transgresses horizon

turns blue

sun transgresses horizon

blue after gold and eternity

sun transgresses

must we figure

sun transgresses

what to do with this motion

sun transgresses

Saint Augustine records 4th century light

almost-lit particles not yet geometric

Saint Augustine confesses to a transgression

light's deliverance to form without pause

television's expended fluorescence

garmentless before the beginning

formlessness without any definition

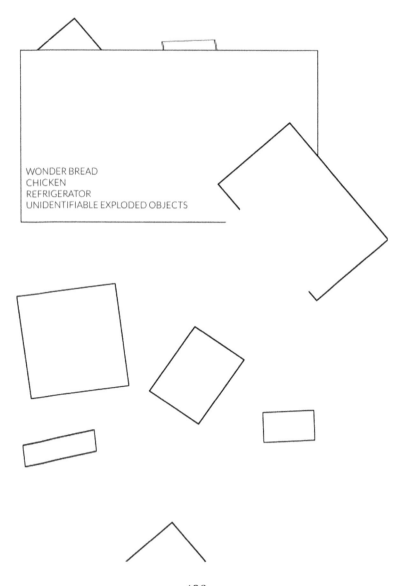

WONDER BREAD
CHICKEN
REFRIGERATOR
UNIDENTIFIABLE EXPLODED OBJECTS

SUNRISE

NOTES

The title of this book is inspired by a statement the artist Joëlle Tuerlinckx made about her work in *Cahiers 2* in reference to a 1994 exhibition in Rotterdam. Confetti, she said, activated the between spaces and allowed her "to do cinema, but in space."

The rectangular diagrams that appear throughout the text are by Emmalea Russo and are drawn from certain moments in the following films:

The Texas Chainsaw Massacre (Tobe Hooper, 1974); I *Clowns* (Federico Fellini, 1971); *Teorema* (Pier Paolo Pasolini, 1968); *House* (Nobuhiko Obayashi, 1977); *Les mains négatives* (Marguerite Duras, 1978); *Trouble Every Day* (Claire Denis, 2001); *Hellraiser 2* (Tony Randel, 1988); *Twentynine Palms* (Bruno Dumont, 2003); *Zabriskie Point* (Michelangelo Antonioni, 1970). The images the diagrams are based on can be found (in the order in which they appear) at: **emmalearusso.com/CONFETTI**

"Honey in Tea" is for Carter Tanton and takes its title from Carter Tanton's song "Honey in Tea" (2021).

"Great Mineral Silence" is for Michael Newton. It takes its title from George Oppen's *Of Being Numerous* (1968): "It is true the great mineral silence / Vibrates, hums, a process / Completing itself / In which the windshield wipers / Of the cars are visible."

SPECIAL THANKS TO Michael Newton, Carter Tanton, Elizabeth Huey, Acyuta-bhava Das, Ariel Yelen, Anna Moschovakis, Abby Nocon, Emily Simon, Kyra Simone, Bridget Talone, Hoa Nguyen, Masha Tupitsyn, Stephanie Leone, J. Gordon Faylor, Òscar Moisés Díaz, Richard

Porteous, Udith Dematagoda, my students, everyone at Café Volan, and to the editors of the following publications where some of these poems first appeared (often under different names and in earlier versions): Black Sun Lit's *digital vestiges*, *The Brooklyn Rail*, *Gulf Coast*, *Forever Magazine*, *La Vague Journal*, *Schlag Magazine*, *Periodicities*, *The Mountain Astrologer*, and *Second Factory*. Some of these poems began as newsletter posts at emmalea.substack.com. *Great Mineral Silence* was originally published as a chapbook from Sputnik and Fizzle (2020).

Emmalea Russo's poetry and writings on film and visual art have appeared in many venues, including Artforum, BOMB, and Granta. She is the author of *G, Wave Archive, Confetti,* and *Magenta* (forthcoming 2023), as well as several multimedia chapbooks and artists' books. She lives in New Jersey and edits the multidisciplinary journal Asphalte Magazine.

www.ingramcontent.com/pod-product-compliance
Ingram Content Group UK Ltd.
Pitfield, Milton Keynes, MK11 3LW, UK
UKHW041901120325
456174UK00001B/11